ALL OUR YESTERDAYS

A pictorial record of the London Borough of Sutton over the last century

compiled by

Ian Bradley : June Broughton : Douglas Cluett

Edited by June Broughton

Published by
Sutton Leisure Services

Introduction

The London Borough of Sutton was formed in 1965 from three local authority areas: Sutton & Cheam, Carshalton, and Beddington & Wallington. These three authorities grew out of communities which, in the mid 19th century, were small, separate and largely rural. The coming of the railways was an important factor in this growth. The population of Carshalton increased rapidly after the station was built in 1868. Central Wallington grew up around the station which was built in 1847, and by 1867 had grown large enough to become a separate parish from Beddington. The New Town development in Sutton began after the station opened in 1847 which, like Wallington, was part of the West Croydon-Epsom line. Photography began in the mid 19th century, just in time to record these and other developments, and the outward spread of suburbia. These changes are portrayed in the photographs included in this publication, which have been selected from illustrations in the Heritage Service's collection, currently housed in Sutton Central Library.

The photographs serve as a timely reminder that not only the general character of the individual areas, but many picturesque and interesting old buildings have been relentlessly destroyed by the march of 'progress'. It is hoped that the formation of conservation areas in the Borough, and the interest and concern of local societies and individuals, will help to preserve what is left of our heritage.

Acknowledgements

Thanks are due to Frank Burgess and Professor Michael Wilks for information and advice; to the late Miss Mary Kempsell for her gift of many photographs by French and Company, some of which are included in this publication; to Ted Evezard for his photograph of the Grange; and finally to all those photographers whose record of the locality have made this book possible.

Introduction to Second Edition

This collection of photographs first appeared in 1977, and proved so popular with the public, it heralded a new era of local history publishing for the then Libraries and Arts Service of Sutton, now part of the Leisure Services Department. Several further collections of historical photographs followed, and a reprint of this one in 1983 also sold out rapidly. This new edition brings some of the information up to date, since there has been a great deal of change in the area over the past fourteen years. Public appreciation of the environment and heritage has also changed very radically since this book first appeared. Sutton now has a Heritage Service which, apart from looking after the archives and resource materials collection, and initiating the local history publications, cares for three historic houses: Whitehall, an attractive weatherboarded building in the Cheam Village conservation area; Little Holland House in Carshalton Beeches; and Honeywood, overlooking the picturesque Carshalton town ponds, which houses Sutton's first Heritage Centre, in the heart of another of the conservation areas which are indeed helping to preserve the historic past, some of which is recorded in these pages.

First printed 1977, reprinted 1983. 2nd revised edition 1991

Designed by Shirley Edwards

Published by London Borough of Sutton Leisure Services, The Old Court House, Throwley Way, Sutton, Surrey SM1 4AF

ISBN: 0 907335 23 3

Beddington and Wallington

The name on the board is Carshalton, but the station is Wallington (though since rebuilt). When the steam railway came to the district in 1847, this was the nearest the line could go to Carshalton, because of land the company was unable to buy. The station was therefore built out in the fields some distance from both Carshalton and Wallington (then a hamlet grouped around the Green). By the time the present Carshalton Station was built, on a different line, in 1868, the new Wallington had begun to grow round this station, and it was renamed.
Note the rambling roses, and the large number of station staff.

The Fords, Beddington, about 1890. At this time only a pedestrian footbridge linked Beddington Lane, to the left, with Hilliers Lane. Other traffic had to ford the River Wandle (it was also fordable from this point down to Bridges Lane). The present road bridge is the second to be built here.

On the left of the river, the terrace of houses known as Wandle Bank has not yet been built. On the right, the footpath is much as now; but the large white house, Wandle Court, has gone. This belonged to the Tritton family - one of a number connected with brewing in the area. A Tritton sold the Ram Brewery at Wandsworth to the Youngs in the 1820s.

Railway Terrace, Manor Road, Wallington, in about 1900. The terrace still stands, though the shop fronts are much altered. French & Co. (proprietor Mr. H.J. Kempsell), the photographers who took the picture, occupied the next to last shop at the left end of the terrace.

'The Old Post Office', Guy Road, Beddington, stood on the corner of Church Lane until 1949, when, having been badly damaged by a flying bomb in 1944, it was demolished. Shown on some old maps as 'The Manor House', it may have been the Manor House for one of the Beddington manors. It was probably fifteenth century in origin.

Latterly it was divided into four dwelling-places; part of it having indeed served as a post-office. The end nearest in the picture was a confectioner's shop earlier this century - note the posters for ginger beer and 'hop ale'.

Beddington House, Bridges Lane, Beddington (near the junction with Croydon Road) in the second half of the nineteenth century, when it was the seat of Canon Alexander Henry Bridges, who, with his father, bought the parkland around Carew Manor (the present public Beddington Park) to save it from the developer when the Carew Estates were sold in 1859.
Canon Bridges was Lord of the Manor of Beddington, Rector of Beddington, and a reputed millionaire. he died in 1891.
The house, after being used in the First World War by airmen from the nearby Croydon (then Beddington) Aerodrome; and then for aircraft disposal and as a builders' merchants headquarters, was demolished in the late 1920s.

'Sunnybank', Woodcote Road, Wallington, which was used as Council Offices by the Beddington and Wallington Urban District Council from 1929 to 1934; when they pulled it down to build Wallington Town Hall in 1935 preparatory to achieving Borough status two years later.
Wallington Public Library was also built on land belonging to 'Sunnybank'.

Instant Tramway: in 1906, a new branch of Croydon's South Metropolitan (later known as SouthmeT) tramways was built from West Croydon to Sutton in six summer weeks. Ten miles of line were laid, and a 'heavy amount' of road-widening carried out; the work continuing day and night to meet a legal deadline. Presumably, therefore, the apparent inactivity of the men in the foreground was for the photographer's benefit.

The shops shown are recognisable today, though the one on the corner of Clyde Road is no longer a dairy. Wallington Police Station now stands beyond the first terrace.

An intentional 'genre' picture from the 1890s, which was a prize-winner for French & Co., of Wallington.

Entitled 'Breakfast Time', it represents a council road-sweeper, whose name is believed to have been Finch, being brought breakfast at work by his wife. The bank against which they are resting was in Manor Road, Wallington, just north of the railway bridge, before Melbourne Road. Large houses, in whose front gardens shops were later built, stood above the bank.

One of the very earliest photographs in existence of any part of the Borough, this shows Beddington Park (now Carew Manor School) before it was rebuilt in the Victorian Gothic style between 1859 and 1866.
In April, 1855, photography was included in the curriculum of the Military Academy at Addiscombe House, Croydon; and this picture is believed to have been taken by a master or cadet soon after.
The house, as shown here, was rebuilt in about 1709 round the ancient Great Hall, and was the seat of the Carews of Beddington: Lords of the Manor for over four hundred years, and a great land-owning and courtier family.

Hackbridge Park Hotel, in about 1920. This had formerly been Hackbridge House, one of the larger houses beside the River Wandle, and the seat of the Goad family, who owned much of Hackbridge in the latter part of the last century. As a hotel, it is said to have had a reputation as a lovers' weekend retreat.

In the Second World War it housed a searchlight battery, and afterwards became a T.A. Centre known as 'City House'. Pulled down in 1970, it stood near Hackbridge Green, by the end of Corbet Close.

Orphan girls posing in about 1900 in the former Great Hall of Beddington Park (Carew Manor).

The food on the table, if it represents a real meal, looks a little sparse.

The Royal Female Orphanage Asylum - the first of its kind in the world - occupied the house from 1866, when it moved from Lambeth, until 1939.

The remaining glory of the Great Hall - its early Tudor arch-braced hammer-beam roof - is not visible in the picture.

Before the trams actually came to the district, in 1906, an earlier scheme was mooted which would have taken trams along Wallington's 'High Street': Woodcote Road/Manor Road, divided by the railway bridge. This photograph and the next are part of a series taken as part of the opposition to the scheme in 1902.
Here we look towards the bridge (not widened until 1964) from Woodcote Road. Ross Parade leads off on the right, with the site later to become the Odeon Cinema, and then a supermarket, on the corner.

Looking back (south) from Wallington Railway Bridge along Woodcote Road in 1902. On the right, uphill, Beddington Gardens (where Sainsbury's now is) leads off. On the left is Ross Parade. Further up on the left can be seen the row of houses known as Rosemount, where Wallington Square and Rosemount Tower are now. Opposite Rosemount is the site of Wallington Town Hall and Library.

Wallington Volunteer Fire Brigade, in Beddington Park, in about 1910. The Chief, Mr. Harry J. Kempsell (extreme right on the fire engine), was also the proprietor of French & Co., the photographers whose imprint the original picture bears.

This photograph, showing Wallington Green and looking towards the new Parish Church, is over one hundred and twenty years old. The church was consecrated in 1867. Danbury Terrace, the parade of shops still under construction on the left, was completed in about 1870.
The Duke's Head, the Regency inn on the right, is little changed today.
As on so many early photographs, doubtless carefully-posed figures have moved during the lengthy exposure of the plate.

Manor Road, Wallington, in 1903, looking north. To the right is Melbourne Road, with the Melbourne Hotel on the corner. To the left, the end shops of Railway Terrace are visible. In the middle distance is Wallington Parish Church - Holy Trinity.
Despite details like the shop fronts, the traffic and the gas lamps, the scene is easily recognisable today.
This photograph was originally published as a Frith postcard.

'Paper Jack', a tramp who dressed in rolled newspapers held together with string (except for his shoes which were made from old car tyre inner tubes) passing the Plough Inn at Beddington. He was a well-known character in the area, friendly and talkative, except when asked the reason for his strange way of life. He is usually said to have taken to the road after having been jilted in love. His real name was Alfred Ellis Preece. He was killed by a car in Benson Road, Waddon, in January 1935.

Old wooden snuff mill on the Wandle at Beddington, once known as 'Sir Walter Raleigh's snuff mill'. Raleigh introduced tobacco, from which snuff is made, and was related to the Carews of Beddington, whose manorial mill it was.
This photograph was probably taken in the 1870s, when it was Lambert's snuff mill. The Lamberts were millers on the Wandle for two hundred years, and left this site for one downstream at Hackbridge before 1878. The old mill-house, much altered, still stands in Bridges Lane, but the wooden mill buildings have long gone.

The Grange, Wallington, was a building which many people remember with affection. It stood in Grange Park, and latterly served as a library, clinic, tea-rooms and reception suite, until it was destroyed by fire in January 1960. It was built in about 1880 by Alfred Hutchison Smee. His father, Alfred Smee, made an experimental garden from 8 acres of marsh which he bought when the Carew estates were sold in 1859. He published a book about it - 'My Garden' - in 1872.
A restaurant now occupies the site of the house.

Wallington Manor House, before 1870, when the seat of William Potts Esq. This was one of two Wallington Manor Houses which faced each other across Manor Road. This one stood roughly where Quinton Close now is. The other, of which no photograph is at present known, stood on the corner of Acre Lane and was called the Old Manor House, although it was not, in fact, as old as this one.
Latterly they were known as 'Black's' (Manor House) and 'Landon's' (Old Manor House) from their last occupants. They were demolished in 1931 and 1930 respectively.

Beddington Corner Church School, Mill Green, Mitcham Junction, in the later nineteenth century. The school was built in 1843 by the Rev. James Hamilton, Rector of Beddington, and served as a chapel on Sundays. It was closed in about 1912, being bought first by Alexander Lambert, snuff miller, and then by the Permoid Glue Company. It was abandoned in about 1926, and finally demolished in the 1930s. The site is now part of the Green, and officially common land.

The photograph was taken or copied by Mr. Tom Francis of Mitcham, who not only recorded by photograph himself from about 1890, but copied earlier photographs of which we would otherwise have no knowledge.

The first 'motor train' at Wallington Station, June 11th, 1906. This was a composite locomotive and coach with the controls linked pneumatically to a compartment at the further end of the trailer car so that the engine, when in the rear, could be driven from there, making reversing unnecessary.

The locomotive is London Brighton and South Coast Railway No.661 - the original 'Sutton'. This class of engine (0-6-0 tanks), designed by William Stroudley, and nicknamed 'Terriers' because of their sturdiness and capacity for work, all bore the names of stations, places or features (like 'Wandle') on the line.

Boorne's Brewery, London Road, Wallington, in 1908. This was Wallington's brewery since before 1810, brewing with water from a spring beside the River Wandle. There are, in fact, two breweries here: the old one on the left and the new one, built in 1904, ahead. 'The Rose and Crown' nearby was the brewery's 'tap' and only tied house.
Boorne's was bought by Ind Coope in 1932, closed down, and sold to Helm Chocolate. The buildings were finally destroyed by fire in 1968. The block of flats for elderly people called 'The Old Brewery House' now stands on the site of the brewery and the brewer's house.

This shop, in Stafford Road, Wallington, is still Gulliver's, and is basically little changed from when this photograph was taken in about 1938; with its coloured Edwardian tiles - many hidden in this picture by the smart little Morris van. The Spratt's signs above, however, have now been painted out, and you can no longer buy 'Best English rose trees' for 6d each, or packets of seeds ('always come up') for 3d.

This delightful photograph was taken in the 1890s. It shows a 'private subscription' water van, used to sprinkle roads to lay the dust in summer, before they were tarmacadamed.

The van is probably standing outside Dr. Cressy's house, on the corner of Manor Road and Croydon Road, opposite Wallington Green. Dr. Cressy was once a very popular physician in the area.

'The Hackbridge', carrying the Carshalton-London road across the Wandle, gave its name to the surrounding (but undefined) area. The Hackbridge shown here is the old cast-iron one, built within two or three decades of the very first bridge constructed from this material, in 1777, at Coalbrookdale. A ford remained beside this Hackbridge, as the picture, taken in about 1895, shows. Predecessors to this bridge were a little downstream.

The present, wider, ferro-concrete bridge replaced the iron one in 1912. The parish boundary ran through the middle of the river at this point, and here we are looking from Wallington across to Carshalton.

The lavender and herb industry was very important in the Mitcham, Beddington, Carshalton and Wallington areas in the eighteenth and nineteenth centuries, and in some areas survived into the twentieth.

The following three pictures show Miller's Peppermint and Lavender Distillery at the beginning of the century. Miller's was at Beddington Corner, and stood between Mill Green Road and Wood Street. Much of their lavender and herbs were grown where the streets of St. Helier are now.

(1) Stacking a cart with bales of peppermint.

(2) Treading down peppermint in a vat.

(3) Bottling operations.

Carshalton

Until its destruction by a bomb in the Second World War, the King's Arms stood on the south side of the High Street. At the top of the building was a stage on which cock fighting took place in the eighteenth century.
The cart on the right of the picture belongs to Mr. Haydon, the butcher, whose shop was opposite the pub.

A Deptford Brewery wagon in the watersplash in Carshalton Pond, in 1897. The wagon was returning from Epsom race course, and towing the card loaded with food, when a shaft broke. The food was scattered in all directions and a relay of small boys waded in to assist in its recovery.

Charles Bone, the last Beadle of Carshalton, who died in 1902. Appointed by the Vestry, the Beadle's duties included bringing idlers, vagrants and beggars before the magistrate and keeping the children quiet in the galleries during church services.

The Oaks mansion, just before the Second World War, when Carshalton U.D.C. had acquired it for use as a public park.
In the late eighteenth century the house was leased to the 12th Earl of Derby, who instituted the Oaks horse-race, named after the estate. The following year, he instituted another race named after himself - the Derby.
The house was damaged in the Second World War, and demolished in the late 1950s.

A delightfully rural Green Wrythe Lane, with farm workers going strawberry picking. It was once called Cannon Sheephouse Lane, from the time the canons of Merton Priory had their sheep folds on Carshalton downs. The road was only made up when the St. Helier estate was begun, in the late 1920s.

A picture palace in Carshalton is one of the attractions advertised on this shop, which stood at the junction of Carshalton Park Road and Pound Street. This would have been Carshalton Public Hall, which was used as a skating rink and, by 1913, when this picture was taken, as a cinema. The shopkeeper was Mr. John Cook, who lived next door at 1, Rose Cottages. Both shop and cottages survived until 1935.

This fine body of men is the Carshalton/Wallington police force in 1892, based at the Police Station in Pound Street, which stood on the corner of West Street, by Margaret's Pool.

The High Street in 1928. The road has been made up, but carcases of meat still hang outside Haydon's. The Haydon family were butchers on this site from 1652, though the shop in the picture dates from the late eighteenth century. Both Haydon's and the King's Arms were destroyed by a bomb in the Second World War.

The Racehorse, West Street, in about 1880. The building to the left is Howson's coach office, the ruined one on the right is a painting shop used by Evans the builder.
This building stood further back from the street than the present pub.

The grotto stream in Carshalton Park in the 1860s, showing Sir Jeremiah Colman (of mustard fame) with his parents, his sister and her governess.
This section of the stream, with the weir, now usually dry, can still be seen alongside Carshalton Place.

Carshalton Park House, also known as Carshalton Place, early this century. Built, or rebuilt, in the late eighteenth century outside the area of the present park, near the High Street, it was pulled down in about 1927.

Catastrophe in Carshalton: a tram lies on its side in front of houses in Ruskin Road. On Easter Monday, 1907, the tram was packed with day trippers travelling from West Croydon to The Grapes, which was the Sutton terminus, most of them intending to picnic on Banstead Downs. The driver lost control of the tram on Park Lane railway bridge, and took the corner with Ruskin Road too fast. Two people were killed, and many injured.

The Culvers, a mid-nineteenth century mansion, which stood in an estate by the Wandle at Hackbridge. In the late 1700s, this land was a bleaching ground, giving employment to many of the local people.
The house was built by Samuel Gurney, who collected exotic wild fowl, including, reputedly, the first black swan to be brought to England from Australia. Such luxurious pursuits were brought to a stop, however, when the family bank failed, and the estate had to be sold in 1866.
The mansion was demolished after the Second World War.

A view down Church Hill and across North Street bridge. The seventeenth century Queen's Well House on the left was demolished to make way for old people's flatlets.
The railings round Anne Boleyn's well can be seen on the corner.

To take advantage of the fashion for bicycle rides in the country, the baker's shop next to the Fox & Hounds became 'The Chestnut cyclists' rest and tea garden', in about 1907. It was demolished in 1913 when the Fox & Hounds was extended.

H. Wardill & Son, Pound Street. The business began as a cycle shop, but Mr. Wardill became an agent for Minerva Motors, and it soon became known as Wardill's Garage. A garage, much extended, still occupies the site.

The High Street looking east, in 1895, with The Square on the right. Holt's premises were previously occupied by another stationer, Susannah Rotherham, who was also village postmistress. She moved to this shop from The Square in about 1878. The shop next to it is Croydon Commercial Gas & Coke Company. Gardners were saddlers in Carshalton for over a century.

Bramblehaw, built in around 1785, occupied the site between Westcroft Road and Acre Lane. It is said to have been built from Portland stone originally intended for the Scawen mansion in Carshalton Park which was never built. Bramblehaw was demolished in 1927.

The shop next to the church dates from the sixteenth century, and may have originally been a priest's house. A carcase rail stood outside the shop between two old trees. When they were cut down, one was found to be hollow, and contained butcher's bills from the eighteenth century, so this was probably a butcher's for nearly 300 years. Now currently a wine bar, using the same name - Woodman, the original butcher's hooks from which meat was hung are still visible at the front of the building.
The building to the left was a water mill, powered by a stream from Carshalton Park. It was demolished in 1907.

The entrance gates to Bramblehaw stood at the junction of Acre Lane and Westcroft Road. Acre Cottage, or Stepney's, on the corner of Park Lane, was demolished in 1927/8 when Acre Lane was widened. A chairmender sits by the lamp post.

A delightful photograph of The Square, taken in 1875, when photography was still unusual enough to arouse the interest of the inhabitants and passers-by.
The gates at the back of The Square stand at the stable entrance to Carshalton Park.

The High Street in 1913, taken from Acre Cottage. A Croydon Rural District Council dust cart stands outside the Fox & Hounds. The Chestnut Tea Rooms are being demolished to make way for an extension to the public house.

The Swan Inn, West Street, c.1870. This building, now largely rebuilt and no longer an inn, replaced an eighteenth century inn on this site called 'The Old Swan Alehouse'.
In the mid nineteenth century, it was the starting point of a daily coach service to the Bell Inn, Holborn, fare one shilling.

In the nineteenth century, Carshalton was well-known for its herbs and lavender fields. This is probably camomile growing in Draper's Field at the Wrythe.

An old cottage in The Square decorated for either Queen Victoria's Jubilee, or for Edward VII's coronation. The building was divided into two, and occupied by William Puttock the deer-keeper and Mr. Radford, Carshalton Park's game-keeper.

William Puttock, the deer-keeper, seated on his deer-cart. He tended the herd which was kept in Carshalton Park by the Surrey Hunt. The deer were taken out, by cart, to be hunted.

The reason so many bowler-hatted gentlemen posed in front of Carshalton Park gates is a mystery. The gates stood at the east side of the park, in Park Lane, and in fact served no useful purpose, as the mansion they were to serve was never built. It was to have replaced Carshalton Park House, the carriage entrance to which was in the High Street.

A view of the Windsor Castle in about 1900, before Beynon Road was built to carry the Sutton-Croydon tramway in 1906. The Windsor Castle itself has remained largely unchanged since it was built in the mid nineteenth century.

Sutton and Cheam

This charming old cottage reminds us of the days when Sutton was a country village outside London. It housed Lucy Green's School, and stood next to the parish church, which can be seen on the left. The photograph was taken in 1865, when the church had only just been rebuilt.

Sutton High Street in 1932. The site of Boots shop is now the town square. The church tower belongs to the Baptist Church, which was demolished in 1934 when the new church in Cheam Road was built. On the right is the Municipal Offices, demolished in 1970.

Cheam Brewery stood on the corner of Ewell Road and Malden Road (since 1922, The Broadway) until its demolition in the 1920s. There is said to have been a brewery on this site since the 13th century which obtained its water supply from a deep well. On the left is the roof of Cheam Court Farm (which is shown on page 46).

The annual staff outing of Webb's the plumbers in Sutton High Street, in a hired horse bus. The photograph was taken in July 1903.

A steam shovel excavating a cutting for Sutton Common Road bridge, on the Sutton to Wimbledon railway line, in 1928. Although planned before World War One, the line was not opened until 1930, when the present Sutton station building was also erected. On the horizon is the spire of St. Dunstan's Church, Cheam.

This wagon, loaded with two-hundredweight sacks of flour, had just returned from Epsom Show, where it had been awarded the cup displayed. It belonged to Dendy Napper, who had steam flour mills and a baker's shop in Sutton.
It is standing before a cottage which formed part of the Tithe Barn. Above the cottage is the tower of St. Nicholas Church.

Cheam Court Farm stood on the corner of Ewell Road and Station Way until 1928: a time when many of the medieval buildings of Cheam were demolished. This farm was a home farm of Nonsuch Palace in Tudor times. The timbers of its barns were used in the construction of St. Alban's Church, Gander Green Lane, called the 'Barn Church'.

Sheep grazing on part of Malden Green, next to the Huntsman's Hall public house in Central Road, Worcester Park, in the early part of this century.

A view of Sutton High Street in 1865, when most of the houses and shops were of wooden construction. The first entrance on the left is where Blackwater Road is today. To the right of it is George Barnes' smithy and ironmonger's shop, established in 1759.

The Cock Hotel, Sutton, in 1898, just after it had been built. The old Cock Inn still stands on the right of the picture, waiting to be demolished. The Cock had been a staging post on the London to Brighton turnpike roads. The Cock sign still stands at the cross-roads.

The shop of Mr. Brown, the butcher, in Sutton High Street, in 1865. The roof over the pavement survived until 1927. Before the days of refrigeration meat was bought 'on the hoof' and slaughtered on the premises.

The third Sutton railway station, built in 1883, as it looked in about 1891. The coming of the railway in 1847 made it possible to work in London and live out in the country at Sutton. Previous to this, Sutton had been a largely agricultural village, lying on the London to Brighton turnpike road.

Leeding's carriage works in Sutton High Street in about 1890. This became Leeding's Garage, which was demolished to make way for the new shop of Boots the Chemist.

One of the series of photographs of Sutton High Street taken by Lewis Hind in 1865. The archway over the road would normally carry the signboard of the Greyhound Inn, a window of which can be seen on the right. One of the trees survived until the gale of 1987 - it stood outside Marks and Spencers.

Angel Bridge, Sutton, in 1932. The wording on the bridge: 'Low Bridge: bus passengers remain seated', reminds us that, unlike the one in the photograph, some buses still had open tops.

Shortly after this photograph of the Old Cottage, Cheam, was taken in 1921, it was moved from near the cross-roads to its present site, because Malden Road was widened to become The Broadway of today. The cottage dates from medieval times and local historian C. J. Marshall suggested that it may have previously been moved from the village of Cuddington in the early 16th century when that village was demolished by Henry VIII to make way for Nonsuch Palace.

Miss Bessie Gardner standing in the doorway of her shop in Lind Road, Sutton, in about 1910. It still exists, though modernised.

The last village smithy of Cheam, established some 400 years ago. It was moved to this site in Station Way in 1860. The building is now a dwelling-house.

Sutton Tithe Barn, which dated from medieval times, and survived until the Second World War. It stood next to St. Nicholas Church, and the site is now occupied by the Central Library.

Looking up Cheam High Street from the cross-roads in about 1912. The building behind the policeman is the Plough public house, and the sign of the Harrow Inn is further along the road. All the buildings in this photograph have disappeared, the Harrow Inn being rebuilt in a Tudor timber-frame style in 1935.

A fine turn-out of hire cars from Leeding's. Behind the cars is Sutton Public Hall in Hill Road, built as a private concern in 1878, and demolished in 1981. It was here, at a school concert in 1907, that Noel Coward made his first public appearance.

Rose Cottage, which stood facing the top of Central Road, Worcester Park. The site was incorporated in Balmoral Road School in 1970.

The site of one of the two Sainsbury's shops which were formerly in Sutton High Street. This one was on the east side of the street at the lower end, the other was on the west side, next to the present town square.

Another view of Sutton High Street in 1865. The house between the two vehicles stood on the corner of West Street. The bar over the road in the background supports the sign-board of the Greyhound Inn, which stood just north of the alleyway beside Marks and Spencers. On the right is Mr. Pearson, the village blacksmith - Pearson's cycle shop is owned by his descendants.

A postcard photographed in 1903 by Frith's of Reigate. It shows Brighton Road, Belmont, looking towards Sutton. Downs Road is on the right, and the old California public house, now The Belmont Carvery Restaurant, is along Brighton Road.

The Queen Victoria in North Cheam, as it appeared in about 1925. It was rebuilt in the 1930s and again, as part of a shopping development, in 1965.

Park Road, Cheam, in 1921. The creeper-covered house is Bay Cottage, which still stands. The charming timber cottages were demolished in the 1960s, and modern town houses now occupy the site.

Sutton's first steam powered fire pump. It was housed under the stage of the Public Hall in Hill Road, part of which can be seen behind the engine.